How News Travels

The Gerald Cable Book Award Series

How News Travels

Judy Katz

Silverfish Review Press
Eugene, Oregon

ISBN: 978-1-878851-25-3
Library of Congress Control Number: 2022952216

First Edition
All Rights Reserved

Published by   Distributed by
Silverfish Review Press   Small Press Distribution
PO Box 3541   800-869-7553
Eugene, OR 97403   orders@spdbooks.org
www.silverfishreviewpress.com   www.spdbooks.org

Cover art: *between us, a current* by Rosie Rudavsky. 2022. Watercolor. Used with permission of the artist.

98765432 First Printing
Printed in the United States of America

Contents

for my mother, Elaine (1935-1989)

and for Oren, Eli, and Rosie

How News Travels

The Other Hemisphere

It shut us up, the new, dumbed us
into silence. And when we finally
spoke from the back seat

of the cab, our eyes glazed
with jetlag, we said, *Those arid hills,
don't they remind you*

*of New Mexico?
And the bougainvillea—it's just like*
L.A. Later, strolling the streets

of Santiago, one of us remarked,
*This neighborhood could be
in Tel Aviv.* It drove them crazy,

our kids, this instinct of ours
to reach for the familiar—as if
there were only one door in

to our middle-aged brains. As if
our need to yolk what was new
to what we already knew

would rob this new place
of its singular
allure. After all, Chile

had been Chile to our daughter
for six months now
and to the Chileans, forever.

We tried to temper
our comments, held our tongues
except to marvel

at the tin-roofed houses
that tumbled toward the bay
in Valparaiso. We walked

our daughter's daily route to town,
watched her select a fish
in the market, take it

from Josephina's salt-withered
hands, and ask in Spanish
the best way to cook it.

Five days later, when we drove
to the Lake District, we began
to settle in. We breathed

the clean air of Pucón. Hiked
mossy forests and parched,
volcanic hillsides. I couldn't get over

how capacious this skinny
country was! Out the window
to the west, a view

of what could have been
Switzerland—*green meadows, cows*—
To the east,

a single snow-capped peak
posing as Mt. Fuji.
I didn't dare say it aloud.

I know they want everything
to be the first, the only—
and it is. Everything *is* the only

of its kind. But also,
after decades of living and seeing,
you discover there are only

so many faces or types
of faces on earth. I have seen
my own mother (long dead)

in the *feria*—
the Argentine version of her—
what she'd look like

if she had lived her life there.
And this, too, is a singular experience.
Have patience with us, Chile.

If you'll just be California
or Switzerland for another
few days, I promise

we'll let you be Chile.
Then we'll carry you with us
everywhere we go.

I.

What the Air Remembers

July. A month that holds
under its sticky wing both my birthday
and the day of Jewish mourning. There in the back yard

thick, shiny leaves seem to rise on their own,
emerald-black hem dragging. One magnolia
lords its smell over the dead grass.

The air in Memphis loses nothing. It is all there.
Grandmother, grandfather, white kitchen counter.
Even my mother's smile can be retrieved, her expression

the night I was conceived. I imagine her body in collapse
kissed in the fall, perhaps a stolen moment
with my father after the boys had gone to bed.

And her hair thick in its first lustre—the one I missed,
the one that disappeared—flickering now like a wing.

First Reader

You sat in ivory bra and half-slip,
your back to me, putting on make-up
while I read to you from the step stool
in your dressing room. You wanted to hear
everything—book reports, essays, poems.
While I read, I checked your small round mirror
for clues. I knew you were interested
if your eyes widened or you raised your brows
out of range. Once—I think it was a paper
on the *Ancient Mariner*—you sat back
in your chair, mascara wand in hand,
and just listened.

Years later, your vision gone,
neither of us could count on your eyes.
I'd walk into a room and find you
listening with your whole body. Now
that too is gone. I still see the dressing room,
your face in the mirror. I still think of you
as my first reader. Only now you're part
of the silent, unseen audience. No eyes, no body…
now I have your full attention.

Season

It is peak leaf season,
a thousand trees about to be blown bare.

Was this the time your hair began to fall
strand by strand onto the white
bathroom floor? It gathered

like fir needles on your sheets
and nested in your drain. The sound
in these woods is deafening.
Each   leaf   brushes the next,
brushes. And when it falls,
cold   branching   silence.

With all that winter brings
nothing so naked
as your bare head.

How News Travels

I used to imagine it like birds flying.
Or a crisp white envelope.
Until now I never conceived of it
nestled inside me, moving how I move.
I step out of the house, forgetting
I am wearing my mother's robe.
It is before dawn; nothing stirs.
No jogger or paperboy, not even the birds
keeping track of things. Am I wearing slippers?
I must be. I move at a steady clip
past the quiet houses on their unlit lawns.
I am taller than usual, held up, afraid
of sudden movement, the swing of my arms.
I walk as if my whole body were filled with eggs,
and my task to deliver them unbroken.
And when I reach my brother's house,
there through the window he is making his way
to the front door to open it
to the news of our mother's death
that I alone have carried in the street
and can finally set down.

The Weight of Absence

When you died our house sank deeper into the earth,
pressing on the roots of trees.
I could feel it sinking
as each visitor pushed open the front door,
laden with cakes and casseroles, the full weight
of their bodies—every muscle and tendon,
shinbone   pelvis   hips   moving
down the hallway, moving past the closet
where your dresses hung, still with your smell,
moving into the living room where our father
sat low to the ground.

I had watched you grow smaller and smaller,
ice chips on your tongue.
And as the morphine took you
here and there, Paris and summer camp,
the lake at night—
I thought I understood:
lighter and lighter
you would become,
a lightness leading
to nothing.

But the house did not rise that day;
it sank.
No mass   no matter
no thing   in the bed
in the blankets
in your place.

Rupture

The week after my mother died, life.
Friends walked in without knocking.
Kisses, whispers, platters to the kitchen.
Do you need anything? What can I get you?
I hated them.
I hated the sight of a cousin's hand in the fridge, an aunt
rifling through drawers for tin foil.
I wanted the sink. I wanted the stools
to sit patiently and wait and wait for her to breeze in
from the back of the house. I wanted the house
to live with her deadness.

The week after my son was born, life stopped.
The news became irrelevant.
Work, sleep, friends fell off the map.
Only his intact body lying on our queen size bed
gazing at our out-of-focus faces
held our attention. The shock of black hair
against the white spread, his bowed legs
cycling through air, tiny arms conducting.
I loved the world's drop from view,
how it could retreat for a while,
how it could die a little.

The Watcher

I would like to trade places with that boy,
go back to the room with the pale blue wallpaper
where my mother's body lay on a single bed.
What was he thinking, that yeshiva boy
sent to watch over her, spell us
for a few hours as her *shomer*?

I'm sure he didn't once look at her
but spoke above and around her
whispering psalms to the carpet,
the bed sheets. I imagine him thanking God
for the small leather book he clutched in his hands
and the thousands of tiny words printed there;
for his tongue to recite them, and his ears
to fasten on every passing sound—
the ice maker turning on again,
one of us upstairs, awake. I imagine
long stretches where he didn't think at all
but, like a night driver, lost track of time
and then, with a shiver, came to.

I would like a turn as her keeper,
the one who stays with the body,
its empty, imperfect shell.
I would like to look at it again,
the body whose touch, for years,
I stiffened against or ignored.
I would like to look at it.

For the Record

After the funeral, Peggy sent a note.
She'd heard you "made your get-away"—
as if you'd thrown a few things in a bag
and off to the next world.
But she didn't see our father rocking
those last hours in the corner of the bedroom.
Or Aaron and me marooned
on the bed with you.
She must not have heard about
the visiting nurse we knew ten days
and trusted more than medicine or blood,
the one who said hearing is the last sense to go
and we believed her, and spoke to you
like midwives at a birth: *Relax*, we said
to your laboring body. *It's okay.*

What can I say—it's trouble getting in
and trouble getting out.
I've seen it both ways.
Is this where I tell you? Sometimes
your absence is a brightly lit field
I am lying in, back against the earth,
afternoon sun warming my face.
Sometimes the wide open space of you gone
is all it takes to let the whole world in.

II.

The Vine

No one tells you the cord of flesh
binding mother and child
is a vine that once cut

grows stronger, unseen sometimes
for whole seasons. Or that one day
it will wrap around you

and your husband in an ordinary moment
as he reaches for the salt
and mentions in passing a phone call

to a woman you do not know. You will feel
a tug   a pull   a cord   reeling you in.
How it will tighten

invisible to your friends, the grocer,
the man on the corner who sits in the sun.
But your husband, he

will feel something catch, a lock of hair
in a low-lying branch, and know
he hasn't got you.

And later, when he takes you up
and loosens your hair and forgives
what is unforgivable,

and your limbs unfurl and your shoulders
and breasts like bound, cut flowers fall—
you will remember

for an instant, the small wound
at the center of your body,
how it withered and fell away.

Urban Renewal

That little Spanish-Chinese place on 81st & Amsterdam
where you asked me to marry you
is gone—
its row of glazed ducks in the window.

Where you asked me to marry you,
I don't remember what we ate;
its row of glazed ducks in the window
our witnesses.

I don't remember what we ate
the night we first met at Man Ray in Chelsea,
our witness
a mutual friend, in town by chance.

The night we first met at Man Ray,
also gone,
a mutual friend in town, by chance suggested
you pick me up outside the Zig-Zag Bar & Grill,

also gone,
and give me a ride in your beat-up car.
You pick me up outside the Zig-Zag Bar & Grill.
You lean across to open my door

and give me a ride in your beat-up car,
that later becomes *our* beat-up car.
You lean across to open my door,
and the rest, my love, is history.

Our beat-up car,
also gone.
The rest, my love, is history.
That little Spanish-Chinese place on 81st & Amsterdam.

Settling

It is the middle of the night.
I am drinking tea, nursing the unsettled
stomach that woke me an hour ago.
For a while, I lay in bed
trying to remember all the women
my friend Jack dated during the six months
he was looking for a wife.

There was blonde Sarah
with the sure, white teeth.
There was Caroline with the tight curls.
There was the translator, the swimmer,
the one whose mother he liked
better than his own—all of them
rounding, one by one,
the turnstile of my memory.

This is a poem for them.
Not the longstanding girlfriends
but the ones who passed through
on a cool autumn night like this one
and brought their glasses of red wine
into the kitchen
to keep me company
while I steamed the beans.

Sooner or later we all slip
into other peoples' lives;
ride the shifts in tectonic plates
that land us
around dinner tables
we never anticipated.
If we're lucky,
for a brief moment
we settle.

Nursing Mother Dreams of Chagall

Something loosens, the grip
of gravity slipping

as sleep approaches. A buoyant
heart rises, wanting

its own view. And why not—here, now
the roof the floor, and heaven there

for the taking. Nothing is pinned down.
I am full of milk, grazing

the night sky for the familiar.
A father's eyes, unreadable as the stars;

a mother's finger tapping
once the house has gone to sleep:

who will talk to me, who
will talk to me, who will talk to me.

I know these people
and even if I don't, I know

my child's cry
can release trough, pig, village store

and set whole towns ablaze.
Give me a yellow cow flying

and I will give you a son's voice
piercing the night,

and in the next room
a mother's milk

leaps, a perfect arc,
to meet his cry.

Smells of the New World

Back in the days when I swelled with milk
and my belly shook like a country fled,
I pulled you in for hours a day, and fed you.

To the north of your head, a tangled forest
of armpit, acrid and sweet, the sour smell of pine.
To the west, around the bottom curve of ballooning breast,
a long, dark crease of salt mines.

Sometimes, if the wind was right,
there would drift in from the east, a raft of smells
from my recent forays: tomatoes or onions or beer,
meat or fish, and always, without exception, fruits—
grapefruits, melons, cherries liquoring your odorless meals
with the distant taste of bounty.

When you were done sucking,
I'd turn you around, slide you along the length of my forearm
and perch you at the far edge of my knees
where you would look out at the world.
And there we'd sit until you burped like a sailor.
Then I'd spin you back around,
let you wash up woozy
on salty shores.

Family Once Removed

        I like to be alone
in the house, but with signs
of family—keys
dropped in the coin dish,
a bathing suit
hanging from the shower head.
That kind of quiet—
a room just left, a solitude
you can swim in
and out of.
        It's like the feeling
I had growing up,
falling asleep Friday nights
in the crook of the brown
Naugahyde couch,
a crocheted blanket
thrown over my head,
lamplight filtering through.
I could hear everything
from there—my brothers
playing Monopoly nearby,
one sifting plastic houses
through his fingers;
and my mother rinsing glasses
in the kitchen,
the dishwasher rack
sliding into place.
I loved my family like that—
at a delicious remove—
their reassuring sounds,
their almost absence.

Autumn Walk

When we pass three hansom cabs on our way into the park,
you say, *You know what I hate about the world—*
People don't treat horses well.
It is a clear day. We can see our breath.
And you have to wear jackets and hats in winter.
Your green cuffs drag the ground as we head uphill.
And you know what I hate the most—
Everything dies. I scoop you up in my arms,
your coltish legs swung over one side, head thrown back.
A shot of laughter flies out of you. And in that moment
I see a perfect row of white teeth, each one separated by a tiny chasm,
and the dirt under your nails and that gaggle of German tourists
taking photos by the pond and the leaves—gold, red, and orange.

Even Motherhood

I turned away for maybe thirty seconds
when she fell from the top step
to the grass—

It wasn't the warm, wet pooling in her mouth,
or my index finger dragging the bottom—

It was the place in the lower gum
I wasn't prepared for

                                  how it gave to the touch
caved in

Bookmark

The way the sheets
hold his shape in the morning,
his smell,

the way her small voice lingers
over the breakfast dishes
though she is at school
whistling.

There is a trail I can follow—
each of us leaves it,
our light impress
on the house,

this place we meet
and depart from,

this book we are all reading
with its silent,
dog-eared pages.

How unceremoniously
we pick up each evening
where we left off,
weave ourselves back
into one story.

What I'm Capable Of

He was no more than three
when I yelled over the rush
of water in the sink
for him to stop bouncing
the ball in the living room, *Stop
now!* Maybe my head ached, maybe
it was late in the day. Done
with the dishes, I went to check
on him. He was standing
in the corner of his bedroom,
facing the wall, perfectly
still. *What's going on?*
I knelt down to my son's height.
A little sound dribbled out
of him, then almost inaudibly,

My heart is going away.

Astronauts

Tucked into the top bunk you call Heaven,
your sister fast asleep on Earth,
you wait for those final moments
before the day's gates close
to hurl your most pressing questions
into the dark... *When did time start?*
Where is everything that died?
One night you said if Dad and I had just been astronauts
we would have understood everything—
as if all the mysteries of living
would be perfectly clear
if only we could get enough distance.

Lying beside you, eyes closed, the night sky
opening within me, I felt myself floating
weightless, and I pictured the earth.
There were no trees or people or bread or cars.
It looked like that photo we've all seen
taken from space—the blue and green sphere
with veils of white around it. I found it wholly
unfamiliar, almost unlovable. In the dark
I felt your skinny arm next to mine.
We didn't say another word that night,
just lay there drifting with our questions.

On Passing the Planetarium

This evening, from the back seat of a shoddy cab,
as we bump along the pitted street where construction
for months reduced this city block to rubble, and its neighbors
to nervous conjecture, where a yellow crane was last spotted
hanging its head in the dirt, we now look under the swaying skirts
of the plane trees and behold, just at our sight line, the planets
themselves—Saturn with its amber tinge, Mercury small and cold,
our own Earth fixed in its watery beauty—all eight accounted for,
lit and suspended in their new pellucid universe, as if late one night,
in some Herculean effort, the long-necked crane shook off its slumber
reached into the heavens and pulled them down.

III.

My Erotic Double

She's got my eyes
but the tightness in the jaw
is gone
and there's no trace
of my mother.
She stands in front of the mirror
like she's the only one
in the room
and when she calls to her husband,
washing dishes
in the kitchen,
her voice is soft
and she means it.
She goes to him,
slides a flat palm
up the back of his shirt,
rests it
on his shoulder blade.

She could write the sex poem.
And it wouldn't even be
the sex poem.
It would be the poem
where they just happen to fuck
before leaving the apartment,
and on their way out
the phone would ring
and she'd go back,
maybe for a scarf,
and not pick up.

Same Bed, Different Movies

At 4 a.m. my husband gets up to pee,
and stumbling his way back to bed
hears me turning, stops in the doorway
and says he's had the most amazing dream.

I was calling you from a pay phone
by the Hudson. It was late
and a blind man was there, waiting.

I'm half-asleep, wrestling
a doctor, or is he a welder? who claims
I have a tumor, advanced—
nurses in little caps—

He picked me up, and I thought he was going to drop me
in the river. But he just held me,
until every ache in my body went away.

Now I'm awake, propped
on one elbow, trying to take in his dream,
but the truth is I'm so relieved
to be out of mine, that all I can do
is look at my husband's backlit form
standing in the doorway
and admire the small movements
of his hands.

The Selfish Heart

Just before my mother died,
I saw her with another man.
He sat at her bedside; they talked.
For those few minutes, her color returned,
her wit, the possibility of living
conversation, words that take you
anywhere. She could have married him.
For a moment, I even wanted it.
But I couldn't keep the thought
of her happiness. I felt panic,
like a child on the wrong side
of a nearly closed door.

I'm Sitting in My Parked Car

telling Melissa how I feel every time I hang up
the phone these days with one of my friends.

The other day, V. was saying how she called the agency
and was shuttled between *Muzak* and the wrong people
for three hours, until she finally reached the right person

to whom she told the whole convoluted story
and asked all of her questions. At the end of the day,
when she relayed this to her husband,

he said, *You mean you didn't get the guy's name?*

Or when B. says, *He thinks I need too much from him.*

Or K. asks, *Why can't he ever just admit that he's wrong?*

There is always a little silence at my end of the phone
accompanied by the ticking of my inner roulette wheel
coming to a stop:

I am the husband.

I am the husband.

I am the husband.

Dressed for the Weather

...and the lands grow distant in your sight,
one journeying to heaven, one that falls...
- Rilke

We could be those lands tonight, lying together
after sex: you falling into sleep through the darkened house,
the shades, the books, your forearm jumping once,
me climbing past to wakefulness, limbs tightening, treetops
clearing, a winter night leaned into—

I had the dream again, the one about the field.
Only this time it was filled with snow.
Tall, choppy snow. And just your black hair
visible over the curve of earth between us.
I remember thinking, for once, I'm dressed for the weather
and how proud you'd be—but I couldn't take one step
toward you. Not even the first step.
I stood there in my heavy boots,
weary with the thought of it.

The Transfer

Where my misery ends
yours begins. I've always felt this

to be the case. I wonder,
is this happening all over

the world? A person turns
to their beloved in bed one night

and says, I feel angry   ashamed
a lion in my throat.

And the beloved holds that
feeling for them. Then

two nights later, the other one
shares some past or present

pain. Here, hold this. And so
it goes. They pass things back

and forth between them,
water in cupped hands,

trying not to spill one drop
in the transfer.

Not a Dream

He's at the door of my sleep   a wolf

crouched by my bed   my mouth

shocked open   like a flower   my body

turned in like a baby   or a book   my nightgown

lifting slowly   like a curtain to a play   I've never seen

but am suddenly,   silently   in

Wake

A white sky ferries its clouds across the city
and now a rain that doesn't so much fall as hang—

heedless who has lived or died that week,
who is walking with a red umbrella

past the quiet movie theater. The heart wants to jump
from an open window, be sprung from this dull

plodding body, body strapped to memory,
memory strapped to shreds of evidence. Once, in Siena,

my husband crouched beside a low brick wall,
afraid of heights, while I surveyed the red rooftops.

It's not important to see everything, I said.
But I was wrong. If I could follow them on their errands,

I would—the man stopping to smell the last
of summer's peaches, the woman turning back

for the dry cleaning. Pick up the groceries. Pick up
the children. Pick up, pick up....

The Duel

I want   and   *I don't want*

are going at it in my head like a couple locked

in combat. I'm rapt and lying

beside you, when your hand   reaches over

to touch my arm. I want   and   I don't want

to swat it away   (*Can't you see*

I'm watching this fight upstairs?)

but your hand has moved to caress   my breast

                                which rises   of its own accord,

pulling my attention

down

into

my body

    as if the brawl in my head, uncontainable now,   has spilled out

into the street

IV.

Questions for My Tribe in Midlife

Was it a cloud or a pillar of fire
that led you lost people
through the desert?

And were you lost,
or merely uncertain
as I feel nearly every day now?

And when you say
'wandered,'
do you mean your time
was unstructured
and so, felt endless—

your looking
brought no pleasure?

And when you looked,
could you see through
the cloud, or was it
like driving through fog
on the Cape?

And the moisture beading up
on your forearm,
was that God?

And the fire
with its bright noise,
did it frighten
or delight?

And how long
would this go on, anyway,
this not being
here nor there?

Shopping

I try on the dress and stand
   in front of the mirror.
       It is and isn't me   the way

the light coming through the rain is
   and isn't ordinary. The way my nine-year-old
is and isn't

young anymore. Just look at his front teeth,
so many truths at once. I turn
   to look at myself

from a different angle, the saleswoman
   smiles from the back. It is and isn't me
   the way *beautiful*

is and isn't the big umbrella
   my husband thinks it is. How does anyone
   ever buy anything? The saleswoman

is headed my way,
   curious, no doubt—how the world is
   (read the newspaper) and isn't

(walk/ river/ fall day) in disastrous shape, and how
   on certain days being in skin can feel
   like consorting with a whole collision

of people, which is why the dress is
   and isn't me, and why, when she asks,
      Do you like it? I don't even know

what she's talking about.

Airborne

In the row in front of me, a family speaking Hebrew
in the row behind, one speaking Arabic—
each with a young daughter.

I am the border between them

here in the two state solution
at 30,000 feet
en route to San Francisco.

The Israeli girl has taken her father's glasses;
she's dangling them over the seat,
her voice rising with the pleasure of over-stepping.

The little girl behind squirms in her mother's lap.
I can feel her foot pressing
into the back of my seat.

We are all of us confined to this small geography,
our holy feet not touching
any ground. Our cities and towns,

spread out and quiet beneath the borderless
clouds, seem not quite real
from here. Even New York

where I live fourteen floors off the ground
and where just last night
I took a t'ai chi class in a room full of strangers

and learned to pour
one hundred percent of my weight
first into one foot, then the other.

Burial

Once I saw my mother
carrying a few forks

and knives
out to the back yard.

Some boundary
had been crossed—

a steak knife
used to cut cheese,

a butter knife
fallen into the wrong

sink. That's how you
make them kosher again—

bury them.
For years I've been carrying

something inside,
a boundary crossed.

You'd never know it
to look at me, just an ordinary

butter knife.
When I'm buried, will I too

be restored
to my former holiness?

House

When they were infants,
I would sometimes be desperate
to be

                  out   in the world, in the air.

A babysitter would arrive
and I would walk a few blocks

                 stunned and thirsty,

nothing

strapped to me—   no harness, no pulling

weight.

                 Within minutes

a grief would well—

               not well up, like water—

it would be a well in me
hollow and deep
and I would turn

and go home.

                 In the Talmud, a rabbi's wife

is referred to simply
as "bayit"—house.

And in the book
my son read in middle school,
the Egyptian goddess

married to Hathor
was called "Mansion of Hathor."
Does a husband have a home

inside the woman?

There are different types
of houses. Permanent,
less so.

       I imagine myself a cottage
with a screen door
and porch.

It's obvious where the idea
comes from—receiver, womb,
tend-er of home

       but if women had made themselves

a metaphor,

would they have chosen
house?

What would they have made men?

Call him money?
Spear?
Marketplace?

And me,   why not boat   river   bird   antelope

From Scratch

As if everything before
my mother's death, is dying.
As if I have to re-make
everything I've ever known.
All the trees—dogwoods,
magnolias. I have to
give birth to my mother,
my father, my three brothers,
take us all back to Memphis,
build the house on Shady Grove
brick by pink brick, paint
the shutters blue. I have to
start the family business, hire
Teenie as head secretary
and the two skinny blondes
who race stock cars after work.
I have to bring the rabbis
from up north, and Jack,
from East Tennessee,
for balance. I have to
send my mother to art school
in the brown convertible,
dirty white top folded back
like a sail, so she can paint
the painting I'm looking at
now, the one from her
Diebenkorn period—no figures,
only fields of blue and green
and around the perimeter
a few graphite lines,
her hand scratching out
a window, a door.

The Sisters

It's the four of them
on the yellow couch at my grandmother's.
Gerry's wearing her crimson lipstick
and my mother, beside her, listens
attentively. When she laughs,
her hair, the color of iced tea, catches
light. Sylvia is there, and Emily,
but I can't hear what they're saying—
I never could. Only their tone,
sharp like a siren. At twelve, I vowed
never to be like them. But oh, their hair
and perfect eyebrows, those whispery
stockings. What I didn't want
to know. *How do you manage breasts?*
Can a baby actually come out of your body?

Once I read about a remote village
in the Hunan province of China
where the women made up their own
language. They wrote to each other
in secret—folded their private truths
into handkerchiefs, scratched out
their sorrows on the hillsides
of fans. Nushu it was called.
Its practitioners never spoke a word
out loud. The men couldn't decipher
it. Even a daughter could only guess
what traveled between
sworn sisters.

Brief Prayer at a Cousin's Wedding

If God is a woman
please don't let her wear
a wig like the one
my aunt is wearing
now that she is religious.

Or a long, brocade dress
that stands still
while the body inside it
struggles to move.

Don't let her fall
for the modesty of the doomed
and dispirited,
the sad or weary
or guilty.

If God is a woman
let her dress like Flo—
turquoise scarf tied at the neck,
hair pulled back
from an open face.

Let the fabric of her skirt
float to the knee.
When she sits down,
please god, let her show
a little skin.

The Appointment

Is this where we'll meet from now on—

                        not the cemetery in Memphis
not the white van with Pennsylvania plates in my dream,
but a doctor's office on 38th and 1st?

I've been in so many like it: the waiting room swimming
with women ill and not, or ill and not yet aware,
flipping with ease through magazines.
The small, dark examining room.
Everything's fine, a doctor says, snapping off a glove.
You can get dressed now.

But just before I do, standing alone
in the windowless, ill-lit room, disposable
robe wrapped around my body, I begin to cry.

It's not that I'm thinking of you.
I'm watching my thighs quiver a little and crying
for living in a body.

Elegy for Peter

for Oren

Two planes   a taxi   a chapel in the woods.
All that travel
and you not there. Peter,
there is a pin prick in the world now, a slow
leak of air, your pulling absence
barely audible. The waves that carried your voice
flat now, our ears still cocked
for their particular sound, *Hey Oren, Hey O.*
that lilt, *Hey O.* the frequency,
the voice on the machine, *Hey. O.* at odd hours.
Just back from the ocean. Hey O., quick question.
Hey O., gimme a call
gimme a call.

How lightly you travelled
this world, shedding clothes
and weight, keys and hair, *Hey O.* hopping
freights *Hey O.* hitching rides, the lines, the flat
lines. I remember one summer at Selma's
seeing your tall frame
stood on its head, legs reaching up
into the night sky.

Your friend, my husband, is afraid
of heights—all that distance.
The long, vertical line
that pulls you heavenward
plummets, for him,
to dirt
and down

through rock and root
and down
to water, *Hey O.* Your sleek body gliding
low and fast, the perfect plane of it
slipping through water, some fissure
we missed, slipping with no one
looking. Butterfly, breast and crawl

through water. *Hey O.*
with no one
looking.

Where does it go? the air, so quick, mid-
stream, mid-sentence, the slow leak,
the flat line.

Anniversary

Everywhere I look I see you.
April again. The coffee sitting too long
in its white cup leaves a ring the color of your straw hat,
the one you wore in the garden. In forsythia, I see you.
The small diamond chip in a stranger's ear.
On the bus I see you, and in galleries and cafés.
Your red coat. I see you young and I see you old.
Imagine, I see you old! Illumined by white hair, you are
drinking juice. I see you in paintbrushes and water towers.
On evening walks, in the broken sky
between buildings, I piece you
together.

It is Passover again.
I see you at the *seder*, your pink and white robe.
In sweet apples and salt water, in the blunt, bitter root.
Tell me, exactly when is the moment
of passing?

I travel to the desert, and there you are—
the low airport buildings are yours; the sudden mountains,
yours. The clear light, the thin air, the hundred
shades of green beside the road. At midday,
the rutted hills are your hands. We drive
and I see them all day long.

I see you as you were, and as you never were.
In charcoal and in flesh, with the unrelenting mind
of Spring, I see you. The petal of the crocus
that clings to my finger, the purple capillaries
sprouting in my leg. You are the pavement under my feet,
the bucket of daffodils the grocer moves
to the front window.

The Haircut

And just like that,
with one haircut,
my husband became
his father.

I could see his skull
through the thinning salt
and pepper of his hair,
his father's skull.

And the bemused smile
that seemed to replace
his own,
his father's smile.

And it occurred to me
that eventually
I would be married
to his father—

a thought
that sent a shock wave
through the whole
thought community

which held
its collective breath for a moment,
as a theater audience might,
waiting to see

how the clever
but trapped protagonist
would escape by a hair
this time.

Day Three,

and the coral peony
on the kitchen counter
has opened into

another life—

last night, flower
now, half- bird, how

did it cross over, how
does it keep opening—

layer upon layer
of petals feathering
fan-like,
deckle-edged,

a ragged softness
with veins
of Floridian color
running through—

if, in three days,
a cut peony
can turn itself

from fist
to flower
to flamingo,

what isn't possible
for this balled up heart?

V.

Dear Mind,

Thank you for sneaking around behind my back
like an industrious lover, arranging things
for the sake of this one moment.

Who but you would have thought of
the bluish-white ear plugs—so simple, so malleable!—
or envisioned them off duty

in two organic shapes,
looking like pearls or purses
or the ovaries themselves?

The morning after surgery, I turned over
in bed, saw the opalescent spheres
on my night table, and thought—

              So that's where my ovaries are.

Who else knows me so well—my ignorance
of anatomy, my willingness to believe
almost anything if it's cast in the right light?

(And that visual reference to the o's in *oophorectomy?* Brilliant.)

But more than anything, mind, thank you
for knowing, when I didn't, that something
was left unfinished, unsolved,

that though the ovaries had lived
hidden in me my whole life, performing
their wondrous storage and release—

they would be gone now,
and gone is different than hidden
and requires its own response.

Thank you for knowing I needed to see them,
however briefly, to say, *hello,*
thank you,   you're leaving?—

these two who had accompanied me
through girlhood, into womanhood
and motherhood.

I needed to take my snapshot
even if the light was bad,
even if I could almost hear them whisper,

It looks nothing like us.

The Niche

If you're not a brilliant artist, it's good to go into one of the professions.
You can find your niche there.
                                        —my brother-in-law

I'm wondering about the niche
I didn't make for myself as a doctor

the little desk that's been waiting for me
in the diploma'd room,

the swivel stool I never tried out,
the patients who've been waiting

all this time to see me.
I never meant to keep them waiting.

By now they've read
all the magazines and newspapers.

One of them has volunteered
to water the plants.

They've formed a small community
in my absence,

phone numbers exchanged,
advice dispensed.

Half of their complaints
have no doubt taken care of themselves.

And one or two still believe
what they've heard about me—

that I have good hands,
and have been known to spend

hours with a single patient.
If necessary, years.

Devotion

My husband says I am *devotional*.
By this he means

I take too long to do things.

Or maybe that I give myself
to things he wouldn't.
On my plate,

an apple. I am devoted to the bite
that makes that *crack*
close to the ear,
a few sprays of juice on the face.

I'm devoted to my walks with Ilene

and to our little café on 74th
that is no longer devoted to its customers
since the French owner sold it,

attending to his new devotions—
a baby, a wife.

The spell brought on
by the third
or fourth poem in a book,

when the noise around me fades—
the place I'm being led,
I'm devoted to.

For years I was devoted
to waking early, making
breakfast for the kids,

running back
while the toast was in
to separate them

from their bodies' devotion
to sleep.

I'm devoted to light—especially end
of day light that oranges
the undersides of clouds,

and to the small gestures
the body wants to make.
I used to pray

in a language I didn't fully understand
and curse the ridiculous
nature of my act.

Now I am devoted
to these same prayers

which wend through me
like old neighbors
looking for familiar talk.

He Brings Her to Me in Florida

I'm poolside when my father brings a mini cassette
he found in the attic.
He's placed the cassette in a recorder,
the recorder in a cardboard cradle,
the cradle in a box,
the box in a plastic bag,
wrapped it all with a rubber band.
The older Latin man
watches from his lounge chair
as I unwrap the package
and hold the recorder to my ear.
Two girls with wet ponytails
fight in the shallow end
as my mother's voice
enters the world again.

It's higher than I remember,
more Southern—so alive
it feels unseemly
to listen. She presses *record*
each time she speaks, *stop*
when she stops, each sentence
released alone, like a parachutist
from a small plane:

It is the day before Thanksgiving.

I just took a long walk.

It feels good to take a walk in good weather…

In less than a minute,
it's over. I keep the recorder
to my ear, listen
through the tape's hiss
for one more
unremarkable word.

Still Life

In a pale green bottle
stand three slender paintbrushes
taken from your studio.
Their silver necks, worn with time—
no longer the smell of turpentine or cigarette smoke,
no perfume. But in their hair, still thick and soft,
a wash of pink.

The Old Economy

It's like a factory has shut down
in the kids' bedroom, all the jobs
moved away. The headboards
and footboards standing
like looms gathering dust,

and the little men on the soccer
trophies, shiny and hollow,
running in place, recalling
some former glory.

But for the life of me,
I can't remember what we made here
day in and day out.

Something from duct tape?
Indian slippers and a banjo?

The painted portrait of Bob Marley
with his dreads
and eyes squinched
against the swirling smoke,
still presides like a benign foreman
from above the radiator,

and a scrap of paper
taped to the bookcase
reads, *It's your birthday—
let's eat pie.*

I miss the hum of the workers,
their idle talk.

Once, in the early days,
I overheard the younger one ask,
What are those things?

She was staring into a shaft
of afternoon light,
mesmerized by the dust motes
floating in it.

That's the tunnel of lint,
the older one said.

Then, as if to save her the time—

You can't catch them,
I've tried.

Sunday in Connecticut

I drive into town.
The streets are damp and breathing,
a few clumps of snow remain
in the yards. Cars parked
in front of the church, and the old
stone library locked in sleep. Behind it,
I take my walk. I listen to the birds
and talk to my mother. I tell her about
my life, but not in words. I just walk
and breathe out what the children are doing,
who they are. She picks it all up.
When I pass the pond and reach
the shady part of the path, where the trees
interlace their fingers at the top—
I stop talking, even inside myself.

To the Old Maples

We caught the end
of your lives and didn't know it,
you who sold us on this house.
We drove up and you were talking
among yourselves, wide-trunked,
stately, not the least bit stuffy.
Gorgeous. Gossiping.
In summer you shaded us, whispered
to each other as we rocked in the hammock,
no one keeping track.
It must be terrible to see each other go
in a few short winters—
even harder than it's been for us
to lose you. I remember the first
ground-out stump in the backyard.
It had snowed early that year
and Mike Root (his real name)
had taken you down. I came outside
and saw a gash in the earth, ground up
pulp, mercurochrome red, bleeding
through the snow.
Then one after the next, huge limbs
sheared off by wind,
crowns cracked and splintering, heavy
branches hanging by the very wires
used to secure you.

Who cooks for you?

my husband intones
in my ear
as we lay in bed
in the country.

You do? I laugh.

No, he says, *that's how you know
it's an owl.*

We hold each other
and listen to the strange call
repeat
at predictable intervals.

Who cooks for you?

Who cooks for you?

And because there is no
response,

only the one voice
haunting
with the same question,

it feels as if the question
is meant for us,

circling us,

Who cooks for you?

Who cooks for you?

As if there will come a time
when the answer will be,

*No one
cooks for you,
No one to cook for—*

and a premonition
overtakes me,   so real

I can taste it for a minute—
does he sense it too?

not a present
loneliness,

one still out there
in the dark.

The Last Five Minutes

Five minutes before the bride
walked down the aisle,
I spotted my aunt among the guests.
Stylish as ever, her small frame
a little smaller. I hadn't seen her
since her husband died.

How have you been?
I asked—

We hugged.

*You have no idea what it was like
at the end,* she said—

        and I thought
she was going to tell me
how hard it was to help
a husband die, especially

at the end
of what seemed like a long,
strained marriage.

It was incredible,
she said.

*It was like we were dating again,
like we were on our
honeymoon—*

her face beamed
as if even she,
who had lived it, didn't
quite believe it.

Wow, I thought.
I smiled and told her
how this proved
my theory
that everything happens
in the last five minutes.

No, she shook her head—
don't you see? All the moments
that came before
were leading to
those last five minutes.

The Necklace

If there's one moment I'd like
to go back to, back to
the feeling of,
it's the two of us
at the kitchen table
dishes cleared, sun
low. You lean in
to untangle me
from the Indian beads
wrapped four times
round my neck—
my favorites,
a single strand
that stretches, unwound,
to mid-thigh. I'm in
a boys' white t-shirt
finishing a beer, you're
so close I can feel
your breath. It feels like
we're in an O. Henry story,
old fashioned somehow,
no telephones or tv,
absurdity and romance
commingling freely
as you unknot
your wife
from her beads
and she, in turn,
reads to you
from a magazine…
one of those endless articles
about (of all things)
Purim—Jewish holiday
of tangled plots,

inversion,
hero and villain
swapping places,
a young girl rising
to secure
her king's ear.
You ply the tiny threads,
cross and re-cross them,
pull a long one through…
it's labor, isn't it, this feeling
we've been here before,
both latched on
to the same trapeze bar
swinging through to the other side.
Those dizzying
contractions, each one
delivered me up
to the sound of your voice,
the story you read
without break, the thread
that would surely lead back
to a world I knew
if only I could hold on….
It's dark now.
You tug and I
lean in, bare feet
propped on the table,
kids, God knows where.
I spin a tale, you follow
a thread, we are
in this together for
as long as it takes,
you and me
and the beads, baby,
you and me
and a thousand beads.

The Room Behind My Eyes

I'm drinking coffee with Melissa
telling her about an idea for a poem called
The Encyclopedia of Small but Significant Gestures,

in which I explore the gesture of pressing my fingertips
against my eyelids when I'm trying to recall someone's name
or remember the word for *elevator*. This small

gesture helps me concentrate. I go into the room
behind my eyes where all the lost things are
and look around for the missing word.

                              And this gesture

leads to a further back room, where my mother and grandmother
and great grandmother stand at the dining room table
scooping the air above the lit Sabbath candles

as if they could bring the light into their bodies,
then cover their eyes with their hands
to say the blessing.
                              And this image

breaks into a hundred images, a mirrored corridor
of all the women before me, back and back
to the first woman

lighting the first candles,
going into the privacy behind her eyes
to look for the first lost thing.

Tulum

I am a good sleeper, a sound sleeper,
but here

             in the curved, blue room

where we've come for my husband's
birthday, he is out like a light

and I can't sleep
for the sound
of the ocean

            whooshing,   *whooshing*

all night outside the windows
and doors,

all night
washing up on shore

            the world,   *the world*

When our daughter was seven
we went to Paris—
dropped our bags
at the hotel

            set out in search of dinner

9 o'clock   and still light—
the women in scarves,
on bicycles,

          r's rolling

over stones
from another century—

You mean this has been here
the whole time?

our daughter asked,
as if all of Europe
were a secret
we'd been keeping from her,

as if beauty itself
were running like a tap

        elsewhere—

Here   the ocean

is

unable to turn off
its aliveness

even for a moment,

when I'm driving or dreaming
or buying lemons
in New York

        it's here, doing this—

whooshing,   *whooshing*

who can sleep
when it keeps arriving

over and over

        the world,   *the world*

Now I Find Myself

                    in middle age.
I entered without checking.
It's marvelous here!
Like an old Soviet road
where they ran out of money
for signs.

                    Look—a woman
walking down the street,
whistling in broad daylight,
her grey hair flying.

Oh, that was me!

Scores of people pass—
no one judging, no one
wagging a finger.

My elders are gone,
my betters have better things to do.

I am under the radar, under the spell, under the veil

of middle age.

I am all gaze.

The world is mine.

One Evening, Years Later

I see the body of my mother over the horizon
expansive finally as sky, a giant
Henry Moore-like figure stretched out
in cloud. No, more like Matisse—languorous,
reclining, arms thrown overhead. I've never seen her
so relaxed. She is done with bones and clothes,
her breasts her own, her belly floating. She is like a woman
who's had her way with the world and rolled over
for a final cigarette in the blue
of the not-world—

     and the earth itself,
small and complete beside her. As if
she gave birth to it. As if
it will be fine without her.

Notes

"The Watcher"—A *shomer* is someone who, according to Jewish law, watches over the body of a deceased person until burial.

"Dressed for the Weather"—The epigraph is taken from Stephen Mitchell's translation of "Evening" by Rainer Maria Rilke.

"Burial"—A brief check on the internet reveals there is one source of Jewish law that says a knife can be made kosher again by plunging it into the earth several times, but this practice of burying utensils is generally considered a misconception with a longstanding, folkloric hold. The accepted way to "kasher" pots and utensils involves immersing them in boiling water. Happily, I didn't know this when writing the poem.

"The Room Behind My Eyes"—*The Encyclopedia of Small but Significant Gestures* is the title of a brass miniature by artist and friend, Christopher Hewat.

"Devotion" carries a dedication to Benjamin Rudavsky (1927-2020).

"Elegy for Peter" is dedicated to the memory of Peter Hutcheson (1956-1999).

"My Erotic Double" owes its title to John Ashbery's poem of the same name.

Acknowledgments

With gratitude to the publications, online journals, and anthologies in which these poems originally appeared:

Bellevue Literary Review	"Anniversary," "The Weight of Absence"
CCAR Journal, Winter 2014	"Astronauts"
Cerise Press	"Day Three," "One Evening, Years Later"
Hanging Loose Magazine	"Dear Mind," "The Haircut," "The Niche"
Lilith Magazine	"Brief Prayer at a Cousin's Wedding"
The New York Times Book Review	"Season"
nycBigCityLit	"Dressed for the Weather"
Plume	"Family Once Removed," "Sunday in Connecticut," "The Other Hemisphere," "Who cooks for you?"
Salamander	"Nursing Mother Dreams of Chagall," "Questions for My Tribe in Midlife," "Rupture," "The Room Behind My Eyes"
The Same	"The Selfish Heart"
upstreet	"Airborne," "Devotion," "Elegy for Peter," "First Reader," "House," "How News Travels," "My Erotic Double," "Now I Find Myself," "Same Bed, Different Movies," "Settling," "The Last Five Minutes," "The Necklace," "The Old Economy"
The Women's Review of Books	"On Passing the Planetarium," "Urban Renewal"
Plume Anthology 6	"Shopping"
Plume Anthology 7	"From Scratch"
Tree Lines: 21st Century American poems, Grayson Books, 2022	"To the Old Maples"

"Anniversary" was reprinted in *The Torah: A Women's Commentary*; "Day Three," was reprinted in *Mishkan HaNefesh: Machzor for the Days of Awe*; "First Reader" was reprinted in *Best Indie Lit New England, Vol. 1.*; "The Haircut" also appeared on *Poetry Daily*; "Questions for My Tribe in Midlife" was reprinted in *Mishkan HaSeder: A Passover Haggadah*; "The Weight of Absence" was reprinted in *The Best of the Bellevue Literary Review*; "The Weight of Absence," "One Evening, Years Later," and "From Scratch" were reprinted in *Mishkan Aveilut: Where Grief Resides*.

Thank you to Rodger Moody for selecting *How News Travels* as the winner of the 2021 Gerald Cable Book Award and for his care and dedication in bringing it to print.

A deep bow of gratitude to my teachers, in particular Jack Baxter (1940-1985) who introduced me to literature, bottle neck blues, and Shelby Forest, and his remarkable wife, Gloria, with whom I've kept the conversation going; Donna Massini, who lit the poetry fire in me; Billy Collins, Marie Howe, Vijay Seshadri, and Dennis Nurkse, whose classes were foundational for me and whose work continues to nourish, instruct and inspire me.

Thank you to Ellen Bass for her generous reading of my book in manuscript.

I'm grateful beyond words to my longtime writing group, Sally Bliumis-Dunn, Theresa Burns, Alison Jarvis and June Stein, for their wisdom and loving attention as readers, editors, and fellow travelers. And to Steve Ackerman and Frances Richey, for not only reading the individual poems in this book but helping me consider its structure as well.

A special shout out to Jessica Greenbaum for the example of her poetry and for championing my work at every turn; to Ilene Sunshine for our walks and conversation that helped seed so many of these poems, and for the inspiration of her own work; to Miriam Ancis for her heart and vision in all things; and to Melissa Bank (1960-2022), chosen sister, brilliant writer, whose hilarious, buoying spirit I will carry with me always.

To the many friends and readers whose encouragement of my work has sustained me along the path, thank you: Chaille Gibson, Bobby Hamburger, Christopher Hewat, Janice Isaac, Karin Katz, Florence Leader, Debora Lidov, Jed Marcus, Kathleen Murphy, Jill Nathanson, M.A. Rocks, Elaine Sexton, Samantha Shapiro, Lienna Silver, Mari Tetzeli, Zoe Ryder White and Lisa Wolfe.

With the deepest possible gratitude to my parents. To my mother for her eye—her art, her life force, her strength of character and joie de vivre. I will always be bringing her the news. To my father for his ear—the music that has always run deep in him, his patient and gracious nature, his storytelling and his unwavering support.

Thank you to my brothers, Joel, David and Aaron, and to my extended family and Jewish community in Memphis who nourished me at the roots and shaped the person I am.

To the whole Rudavsky clan, appreciators and encouragers all, thank you for your interest and your love.

Finally to Oren, partner in art and life, for his documentarian's eye and willing heart, his unfailing encouragement of my work. I'm so grateful to be going through this life with you.

And to Eli and Rosie, poems unfolding in real time. You inspire me daily with your own wild and beautiful creativity.

About the Author

Judy Katz's poems have appeared on *Poetry Daily* and in *The New York Times Book Review*, *Salamander*, *The Women's Review of Books*, *Plume*, *upstreet*, and other print and online journals. Her work has been nominated for a Pushcart Prize and widely anthologized, appearing in such publications as *Best Indie Lit New England*, *The Best of the Bellevue Literary Review* and *Tree Lines: 21st Century American Poems*. Judy graduated from Barnard College and received an MFA in poetry from Sarah Lawrence College. For many years, she worked as a documentary filmmaker and producer of public television. Judy currently teaches poetry in New York City.

The interior text and display type were set in Adobe Jenson, a faithful electronic version of the 1470 roman face of Nicolas Jenson. Jenson was a Frenchman employed as the mintmaster at Tours. Legend has it that he was sent to Mainz in 1458 by Charles VII to learn the new art of printing in the shop of Gutenberg, and import it to France. But he never returned, appearing in Venice in 1468; there his first roman types appeared, in his edition of Eusebius. He moved to Rome at the invitation of Pope Sixtus IV, where he died in 1480.

Type historian Daniel Berkeley Updike praises the Jenson Roman for "its readability, its mellowness of form, and the evenness of color in mass." Updike concludes, "Jenson's roman types have been the accepted models for roman letters ever since he made them, and, repeatedly copied in our own day, have never been equalled."

The type used on the front cover is Legato regular and Legato italic. The type for the title and author name on the spine is Legato. Designed for legibility, its essential attribute is that the black of the individual letterforms is made equal in importance to the white inside and between the letters. By making the black and white harmonize, Legato approaches an ideal of readability, since reading involves the perception of positive/negative space as one thing. The type used for the back cover text and for the press name on the spine is Adobe Garamond Pro. Designed by Robert Slimbach (1989) and Claude Garamond ((1499-1561), Adobe Garamond is a digital interpretation of the roman types of Claude Garamond and the italic types of Robert Granjon. Adobe type designer Robert Slimbach has captured the beauty and balance of the original Garamond typefaces.

Cover design by Nita Ybarra, NYDesign/SF
Text design by Rodger Moody and Connie Kudura, ProtoType
Printed on acid-free papers and bound by McNaughton & Gunn